W9-BJO-531

H00

For Love's Sake Only

For Love's Sake Only

SONGS
OF THE HEART
BY
ELIZABETH BARRETT
AND
ROBERT BROWNING

Selected by Benjamin Whitley

HALLMARK EDITIONS

PHOTOGRAPHS
W. Galen Barton: Page 45; Rev. Herman A. Bielenberg:
Page 33; Colour Library International: Page 15; Jim Cozad:
Page 36-37; Phoebe Dunn: Page 27; Richard Fanolio: Pages
7 and 28-29; Richard Fanolio/Phil Smith: Page 4-5; Harv
Gariety: Cover, Pages 35 and 43; Carol Hale: Pages 10-11
and 40-41; Maxine Neil Jacobs (Photographed at the Bell-
ingrath Gardens, Alabama): Page 17; Jack Jonathan: Page
18-19; Joseph Klemovich: Page 25; Jim Lipp: Page 31;
Plessner International Incorporated: Page 12; H. Arm-
strong Roberts: Page 39; Daniel R. Schiffer: Page 23; Otto
Storch: Pages 8 and 21; Sam Zarember: Title Page.

Set in Baskerville, the fine transitional face
named for the 18th century English printer
John Baskerville of Birmingham.
Printed on Hallmark Crown Royale paper.
Designed by Joel Ravitch.

For Love's
Sake
Only

YOU'LL LOVE ME YET
By Robert Browning

You'll love me yet!—and I can tarry
  Your love's protracted growing:
June reared that bunch
    of flowers you carry
  From seeds of April's sowing....

I plant a heartful now: some seed
  At least is sure to strike,
And yield—
    what you'll not pluck indeed,
  Not love, but, may be, like....

You'll look at least
    on love's remains,
  A grave's one violet:
Your look? —
    that pays a thousand pains.
  What's death? You'll love me yet!

...LOVE, MERE LOVE, IS BEAUTIFUL INDEED

By Elizabeth Barrett Browning

...Love, mere love, is beautiful indeed
And worthy of acceptation.
     Fire is bright,
Let temple burn, or flax; an equal light
Leaps in the flame
     from cedar-plank or weed:
And love is fire....

And when I say at need
I love thee...mark!...I love thee—
    in thy sight
I stand transfigured, glorified aright,
With conscience of the new rays
    that proceed
Out of my face toward thine....

There's nothing low
In love, when love the lowest:
meanest creatures
Who love God,
God accepts while loving so.
And what I feel,
across the inferior features
Of what I am,
doth flash itself, and show
How that great work of Love
enhances Nature's.

LIFE IN A LOVE
By Robert Browning

Escape me?

Never —

Beloved!

While I am I, and you are you,

　So long as the world

　　contains us both,

　Me the loving and you the loth,

While the one eludes,

　　must the other pursue....

My life is a fault at last, I fear:
It seems too much like a fate, indeed!
Though I do my best
I shall scarce succeed. . . .

But what if I fail of my purpose here?
It is but to keep the nerves at strain,
  To dry one's eyes and laugh at a fall,
And, baffled, get up and begin again,—
  So the chase takes up one's life,
    that's all....

While, look but once
    from your farthest bound
  At me so deep in the dust and dark,
No sooner the old hope goes to ground
  Than a new one,
    straight to the self-same mark,
I shape me—
Ever
Removed!

BELOVÈD, MY BELOVÈD

By Elizabeth Barrett Browning

Belovèd, my Belovèd, when I think
That thou wast in the world a year ago,
What time I sat alone here in the snow
And saw no footprint,
        heard the silence sink
No moment at thy voice...

...but, link by link,
Went counting all my chains as if that so
They never could fall off at any blow
Struck by thy possible hand,
    —why, thus I drink
Of life's great cup of wonder!...

Wonderful,
Never to feel thee thrill the day or night
With personal act or speech,
    — nor ever cull
Some prescience of thee
    with the blossoms white
Thou sawest growing!
    Atheists are as dull,
Who cannot guess
    God's presence out of sight.

LOVE
By Robert Browning

So, the year's done with!
   (Love me for ever!)
All March begun with,
   April's endeavour;
May-wreaths that bound me
   June needs must sever;
Now snows fall round me,
   Quenching June's fever—
   (Love me for ever!)

IF THOU MUST LOVE ME
By Elizabeth Barrett Browning

If thou must love me, let it be for nought
Except for love's sake only. Do not say
'I love her for her smile—
        her look—her way
Of speaking gently,—
        for a trick of thought
That falls in well with mine,
        and certes brought
A sense of pleasant ease on such a day'—
For these things in themselves,
        Belovèd, may
Be changed, or change for thee,—
        and love, so wrought,
May be unwrought so....

Neither love me for
Thine own dear pity's
        wiping my cheeks dry,—
A creature might forget to weep,
        who bore
Thy comfort long,
        and lose thy love thereby!...

*But love me for love's sake, that evermore
Thou mayst love on,
through love's eternity.*